Multi-Jurisdictional Mitigation Planning

State and Local Mitigation Planning
How-To Guide Number Eight
FEMA 386-8 *August 2006*

 FEMA

U.S. Department of Homeland Security
500 C Street, SW
Washington, DC 20472

TABLE OF CONTENTS

The Department of Homeland Security's Federal Emergency Management Agency (FEMA) has developed a series of **"how-to" guides** for the purpose of assisting Tribes, States, and local governments in developing effective hazard mitigation planning processes. The material presented in these guides is intended to address the needs of both large and small communities with varying degrees of technical expertise and financial resources.

The topic area for this guide is "Multi-Jurisdictional Approaches to Hazard Mitigation Planning" (FEMA 386-8). This guide provides suggestions to local governments in preparing multi-jurisdictional hazard mitigation plans that meet the DMA 2000 planning requirements. Other guides that have been developed by FEMA as part of the "how-to" series include:

- Getting started with the mitigation planning process, including important considerations for how you can organize your efforts to develop an effective mitigation plan (FEMA 386-1);
- Identifying hazards and assessing losses to your community, State, or Tribe (FEMA 386-2);
- Setting mitigation priorities and goals for your community, State, or Tribe and writing the plan (FEMA 386-3);
- Implementing the mitigation plan, including project funding and maintaining a dynamic plan that changes to meet new developments (FEMA 386-4);
- Evaluating potential mitigation actions through the use of benefit-cost review (FEMA 386-5) (to be published);
- Incorporating special considerations into hazard mitigation planning for historic properties and cultural resources, the topic of this how-to guide (FEMA 386-6);
- Incorporating mitigation considerations for manmade hazards into hazard mitigation planning (FEMA 386-7); and
- Finding and securing technical and financial resources for mitigation planning (FEMA 386-9) (to be published).

The first four guides are commonly referred to as the "core four" as they provide a broad overview of the core elements associated with hazard mitigation planning. This and the other guides are supplementary "how-to" guides that are to be used in conjunction with the "core four." The how-to guides can be ordered (free of charge) by calling 1-800-480-2520, or they can be downloaded from the FEMA site at http://www.fema.gov/plan/mitplanning/planning_resources.shtm.

Disaster Mitigation Act of 2000 (DMA 2000)
DMA 2000 provides an opportunity for States, Tribal Governments, and local jurisdictions to significantly reduce their vulnerability to natural hazards. It also allows them to streamline their access to and use of Federal disaster assistance,

through pre-disaster hazard mitigation planning. DMA 2000 places new emphasis on State, Tribal, and local mitigation planning by requiring these entities to develop and submit mitigation plans as a condition of receiving various types of pre- and post-disaster assistance (such as the Pre-Disaster Mitigation Program [PDM] and the Hazard Mitigation Grant Program [HMGP]) under the Stafford Act.

On February 26, 2002, FEMA published under Title 44 Part 201 of the Code of Federal Regulations (CFR) an **Interim Rule** (the Rule) to implement the mitigation planning requirements of DMA 2000. The Rule outlines the requirements for both State and local mitigation plans. FEMA has prepared a document, **Multi-Hazard Mitigation Planning Guidance under the Disaster Mitigation Act of 2000**, that explains the requirements of the Rule with the help of sample plan excerpts and discussion. It can be downloaded from http://www.fema.gov/plan/mitplanning/guidance.shtm, or can be obtained from FEMA regional offices.

What is a Multi-Jurisdictional Hazard Mitigation Plan?

A multi-jurisdictional hazard mitigation plan is a plan jointly prepared by more than one jurisdiction. The term "jurisdiction" in this guide means "local government." Title 44 Part 201 Mitigation Planning in the CFR defines a "local government" as "any county, municipality, city, town, township, public authority, school district, special district, intrastate district, council of governments (regardless of whether the council of governments is incorporated as a nonprofit corporation under State law), regional or interstate government entity, or agency or instrumentality of a local government; any Indian tribe or authorized tribal organization, or Alaska Native village or organization; and any rural community, unincorporated town or village, or other public entity."

Why Conduct Multi-Jurisdictional Hazard Mitigation Planning?

Local jurisdictions have the option of preparing a multi-jurisdictional hazard mitigation plan under DMA 2000. Jurisdictions can benefit in several ways when they choose to participate in a multi-jurisdictional planning process. Among such benefits, this process:
- enables comprehensive approaches to mitigation of hazards that affect multiple jurisdictions;
- allows economies of scale by:
  - leveraging individual capabilities; and
  - sharing costs and resources;
- avoids duplication of efforts; and
- imposes an external discipline on the process.

A multi-jurisdictional planning approach may have certain complications that jurisdictions should consider before joining a collective planning effort. Some potential challenges include:
- having less individual control over the process;
- needing strong, centralized leadership and organizational skills;
- dealing with conflict that may arise among participants; and,
- requiring consistent participation by each jurisdiction throughout the planning process so that the plan stays on schedule.

Each jurisdiction should consider whether the advantages in participating in a joint planning effort outweigh the disadvantages for its particular situation. Jurisdictions must understand that when opting to participate in a multi-jurisdictional plan, they still must meet all planning requirements in the Rule, including formal adoption of the plan. Failure of any of the participating jurisdictions to meet the requirements will not prevent the compliant jurisdictions from adopting the plan, getting it approved by FEMA, and consequently being eligible for project grants.

FEMA's Flood Mitigation Assistance (FMA) Program

The FMA program has specific, flood-related planning. When preparing a multi-jurisdictional mitigation plan, the Planning Team must address the following FMA planning requirements if the community intends to apply for FMA project grants:

1. In the risk assessment section, under Assessing Vulnerability – Identifying Structures, §201.6(c)(2)(ii)(A), the plan **must** include a section that identifies the number and describes the type (residential or commercial) of repetitive loss properties in the community; and,

2. In the mitigation strategy section, under implementation of Mitigation Actions, §201.6(c)(3)(iii), the plan **must** include documentation that continued enforcement of applicable floodplain management standards is part of its strategy for reducing flood losses.

How Do You Organize a Multi-Jurisdictional Plan?

There are a variety of ways that multi-jurisdictional plans may be organized. For example, they may describe what is common to all jurisdictions in one section of the plan and then have for each participating jurisdiction an appendix containing a detailed description of each jurisdiction (e.g., its history, economy, demographics, etc.), specific hazard information, and a mitigation strategy the jurisdiction commits to implementing. Figure 1 depicts this conceptual organization of a multi-jurisdictional plan. Jurisdictions can ask their State Hazard Mitigation Officer (SHMO) for a copy of an approved plan that can serve as a guide for assembling their own mitigation plan.

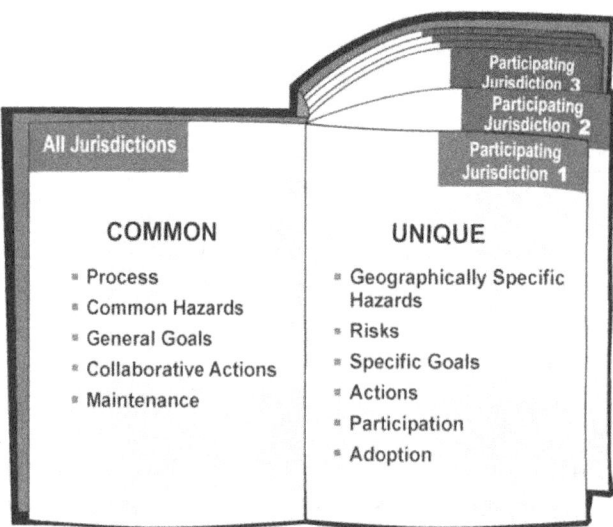

Figure 1. Conceptual Organization of a Multi-Jurisdictional Plan

About This Document

This how-to guide uses the Plan Review Crosswalk (the Crosswalk) to explain each of the Rule's planning requirements. The Crosswalk is a checklist FEMA uses to (1) determine whether a plan meets the Rule's planning requirements and (2) provide comments to jurisdictions. The Crosswalk can be found in the FEMA publication "Multi-Hazard Mitigation Planning Guidance under the Disaster Mitigation Act of 2000," referred to on page ii of the Foreword. The Crosswalk may be downloaded from http://www.fema.gov/plan/mitplanning/guidance.shtm. More detailed guidance on preparing a plan can be found in the "core four" how-to guides, identified on page ii of the Foreword. This guide should be used as a companion to those more detailed guides.

This how-to guide provides the following:
- The Rule language – From the CFR and italicized in this guide.
- Reviewer's Comments – Revisions to address the planning requirements, presented in the form of questions under the column titled Elements in the Crosswalk. The comments are of two types:
  - "Required," which specify the revisions jurisdictions must make to meet the specific language of the Rule; and
  - "Recommended," which encourage jurisdictions to go beyond the minimum requirements, thus preparing a more comprehensive plan.
- Tips – Recommendations for how to meet the specific requirements. These tips suggest ways to address the Reviewer's Comments.
- Exhibits – Worksheets to assist the Planning Team in collecting and organizing necessary plan information. Sample worksheets provided in the body of this guide use an alternate font to illustrate how the exhibits can be completed. Blank worksheets are included in the Appendix.

Key Principle

The key principle underlying multi-jurisdictional planning, and followed in this how-to guide is that whenever the Rule refers to a jurisdiction, the requirement is applicable to each participating jurisdiction.

As discussed in FEMA's publication, *Getting Started: Building Support for Mitigation Planning* (FEMA 386-1), adoption of the plan solidifies the local governments' commitment to implement the plan and keep it alive with updates.

Multi-Jurisdictional Plan Adoption

Plan Review Evaluation Criteria

Requirement §201.6(c)(5): *For multi-jurisdictional plans, each jurisdiction requesting approval of the plan must document that it has been formally adopted.*

Element	Typical Reviewer's Comments
A. Does the plan indicate the specific jurisdictions represented in the plan?	**Required** • List the jurisdictions requesting approval of the plan. **Recommended** • List all jurisdictions and, for county (or other encompassing jurisdictions such as a township or parish) plans, indicate which ones are participating in this multi-jurisdictional planning process and which are preparing their own plans.
B. For each jurisdiction, has the local governing body adopted the plan?	**Required** • Each participating jurisdiction must adopt the plan to receive formal approval from FEMA. • List the status of adoption for each of the participating jurisdictions.
C. Is supporting documentation, such as a resolution, included for each participating jurisdiction?	**Required** • For each participating jurisdiction requesting approval of the plan, include supporting documentation.

TIP 1 – Identify potential participants and invite them to the planning process

The first order of business when initiating a multi-jurisdictional planning process is to determine who will participate in the plan. Consider the definition of local government on page 1 and list all the potential participating jurisdictions. Invite them to join in the planning process and describe your efforts to involve them in the plan, even if some of those jurisdictions do not end up participating in the plan.

Contact all Indian Tribal Governments in your geographic area regarding their preference for plan participation. Indian Tribal Governments may contact FEMA Regions for guidance on participation in a multi-jurisdictional plan.

Invite universities and colleges to participate in the multi-jurisdictional plan. (Publicly funded universities and colleges will need to have their own plan or participate in a multi-jurisdictional plan if they intend to apply for hazard mitigation project grants under FEMA's Pre-Disaster Mitigation Program.)

TIP 2 – Clearly identify the participants in the plan

Clearly and explicitly identify the <u>participating</u> jurisdictions.

Also identify all jurisdictions within the geographic planning area that have chosen not to participate, those who participated but did not fully comply with all the participation requirements, and those jurisdictions that are not participating because they are preparing their own plans. Providing the participation status of all jurisdictions in the geographic planning area leaves no doubt about who is participating in the plan.

TIP 3 – Include a map locating the participants

Include a map showing all the jurisdictions within the geographic bounds of the plan and indicate which ones are participating/not participating in the plan. Clearly show the jurisdictional boundaries.

TIP 4 – Include copies of adoption resolutions

When submitting the plan for formal FEMA approval, include a photocopy of the signed resolution of adoption for each jurisdiction. Note that "approval" by local officials is not the same as formal "adoption." FEMA requires that jurisdictions <u>adopt</u> the plan.

Do not adopt the plan before first submitting a draft for FEMA to conduct a review (see Tip 7). Include a draft of the resolution in the draft plan to illustrate the wording of the adoption resolution.

TIP 5 – Use a uniform resolution

The Plan Author should provide a sample resolution to all participants, encouraging them to use standard language to the maximum practical extent. When each individual jurisdiction develops its own resolution of adoption there may be some inadvertent omissions.

The resolution must clearly state that the participating jurisdiction is adopting the plan. Use of the word **approve** instead of **adopt** does not meet the adoption requirement. A sample resolution is included as Exhibit 1.

Sample Exhibit 1: Adoption Resolution

(Name of Jurisdiction)   Town A

(Governing Body)   Town Council

(Address)   100 Main Street, Town A

RESOLUTION

WHEREAS, the County ABC Multi-Hazard Mitigation Plan has been prepared in accordance with FEMA requirements at 44 C.F.R. 201.6; and,

WHEREAS, Town A, participated in the preparation of a multi-jurisdictional plan, County ABC Multi-Hazard Mitigation Plan; and,

WHEREAS, Town A is a local unit of government that has afforded the citizens an opportunity to comment and provide input in the Plan and the actions in the Plan; and

WHEREAS, Town A has reviewed the Plan and affirms that the Plan will be updated no less than every five years.

NOW THEREFORE, BE IT RESOLVED by Town Council that Town A adopts the County ABC Multi-Hazard Mitigation Plan as this jurisdiction's Multi-Hazard Mitigation Plan, and resolves to execute the actions in the Plan.

ADOPTED this XX day of December, 20XX at the meeting of the Town Council.

_____

(Mayor)

TIP 6 – Provide alternate acceptable forms of adoption documentation

If you plan on using some documentation other than an adoption resolution, consult with your State Hazard Mitigation Officer (SHMO) before you submit your plan for approval.

Some multi-jurisdictional plans have chosen other ways to document the adoption of the plan. A single resolution with signatures of authorized representatives from the participating jurisdictions has been considered acceptable. A statement in the plan that the resolutions are available on file has also been considered acceptable, with the condition that each participating jurisdiction's name and date of adoption be listed in the plan.

If a local jurisdiction has not passed a formal resolution, or used some other documentation of adoption, the clerk of the governing body or city attorney must provide written confirmation that the action meets their legal requirements for official adoption, and/or the highest elected local official or their designee must submit written proof of adoption. The signature of one of these officials is *required* with the explanation or other proof of adoption.

Minutes of a council or other meeting during which the plan is adopted *may or may not* be sufficient – depending on the local law. That is why, if minutes are being submitted as documentation of adoption of the plan, the clerk of the governing body, or city attorney, must provide a brief, written explanation, such as, "In accordance with section X of the city code/ordinances, this constitutes formal adoption of the measure." Their signature with the explanation would be sufficient. In the case of meeting minutes, it must be clear that the plan was adopted at that meeting.

TIP 7 – Send a draft plan for review

Most plans submitted for the first time are returned with comments and required revisions. If the plan was adopted prior to submission, any revisions made to it will likely require that the plan be re-adopted. Therefore, FEMA recommends that local mitigation plans be submitted for review prior to adoption. Once FEMA determines that the plan is approvable, the plan can be adopted and a copy submitted through the State to FEMA to receive formal approval.

As discussed in the FEMA publication *Getting Started: Building Support for Mitigation Planning* (FEMA 386-1), participation in the planning process is essential to the success of the plan.

Multi-Jurisdictional Planning Participation

Plan Review Evaluation Criteria
Requirement §201.6(a)(3): *Multi-jurisdictional plans (e.g., watershed plans) may be accepted, as appropriate, as long as each jurisdiction has participated in the process ... Statewide plans will not be accepted as multi-jurisdictional plans.*

Element	Typical Reviewer's Comments
A. Does the plan describe **how** each jurisdiction participated in the plan's development?	**Required** ▪ Describe how <u>each</u> jurisdiction participated in the planning process.

TIP 8 – Participation by multiple jurisdictions

The second order of business is to create a structure for communication and decision-making. Team members should agree upon who will be responsible for the overall plan development and identify a responsible point of contact for each participating jurisdiction. Whatever organization or approach is used, it is essential that some structure for accountability be developed at the onset of the process. The organizational models below have a:

- "Plan Author" who coordinates and may do much of the work in preparing the plan. This may be a County agency, regional planning commission, university, or a consultant with the staff and capability to do research, prepare maps, develop text, and orchestrate the actual production of the plan document. Sometimes the author is a public agency which exercises leadership while relying on technical support from outside consultants.

- "Planning Team" (in most cases) to assist the Plan Author and represents the jurisdictions in the preparation of the plan. Using a team fosters collaboration, develops a "corporate memory" of the process, and may provide a structure for plan maintenance. For details on building a Planning Team, refer to Chapter 2 of *Getting Started: Building Support for Mitigation Planning* (FEMA 386-1).

TIP 9 – Include team members with technical and community knowledge

Jurisdictions should carefully consider who represents them in the planning process. Although interested citizens and elected officials may be available, it is very helpful to include the municipal engineer, planner, emergency manager, or other individuals who have an in-depth understanding of the jurisdiction's risks and capabilities.

TIP 10 – Encourage representatives to see the planning process to completion

Try to keep the same people involved through the entire planning process. Changing team members can slow meetings as the team explains the background on issues. When team members cannot be expected to attend all the meetings, have them identify an alternate at the onset of the planning process. Team members should keep their alternates regularly informed so that their alternates are ready to actively participate in discussions and make decisions.

There is no single organizational model that will work best for all jurisdictions. This how-to guide describes two organizational models and an example of how the two can be combined into a third model. Select one that most closely fits with your capabilities. Whichever you choose, all participating jurisdictions must agree on the structure, follow an agreed-upon schedule, and comply with the agreed upon participation components (see Tip 13).

Direct Representation Model

In the first model for the multi-jurisdictional plan organization, each participating jurisdiction has direct representation on the Planning Team (see Figure 2). The representatives act on the jurisdiction's behalf and bear the responsibility to be a conduit between the Plan Author and the jurisdiction. Because of the direct representation, the individual jurisdictions are able to be fully engaged in developing all aspects of the plan.

This model works best where the number of participants is relatively few and representatives are actively engaged in the process. Because of the direct involvement, the plan should be highly reflective of the unique needs and interests of the individual jurisdictions.

PLAN AUTHOR
Coordinates plan preparation and participation

PLANNING TEAM
of
DIRECT REPRESENTATIVES

| PARTICIPATING JURISDICTION | PARTICIPATING JURISDICTION | PARTICIPATING JURISDICTION | PARTICIPATING JURISDICTION |

Figure 2. Direct Representation Model

Authorized Representation Model

In the second model, individual jurisdictions may authorize the Plan Author to prepare the plan on their behalf (see Figure 3). The jurisdictions should formally authorize the Plan Author or some other party to act on their behalf in developing the plan. (A sample resolution granting the Plan Author the authority to act on behalf of the jurisdiction is found in Exhibit 2.)

This model is most appropriate where participants have little capability for active participation in the process. An example might be where a county agency prepares a plan that includes several small towns or incorporated jurisdictions that have no staff experienced in preparing plans.

The benefits of this model are that it has few coordination issues and it can provide support to jurisdictions without sufficient capacity to otherwise participate in the mitigation planning process. However, this model minimizes the direct involvement of the jurisdictions and may not be fully reflective of each jurisdiction's concerns, interests, and goals.

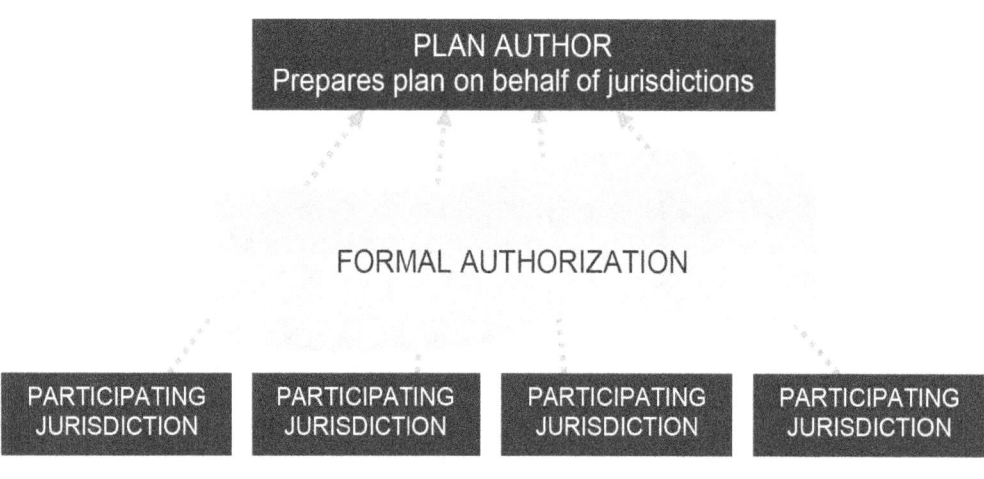

Figure 3. Authorized Representation Model

In the draft stage, the Plan Author (acting as the authorized representative) must seek public involvement and comments and should communicate with the governing body of each jurisdiction. The Plan Author thus serves as a facilitator of the planning process.

TIP 11 – Use formal authorizations

Formal authorization is clear evidence to the plan reviewer that the jurisdiction is utilizing this method of participation. This removes any question regarding how the jurisdiction has met the participation criteria.

Sample Exhibit 2: Resolution for Authorized Representation
Resolution for authorizing the Plan Author to act on behalf of Local Jurisdiction

(Name of Jurisdiction) Town A

(Governing Body) Town Council

(Address) 100 Main Street, Town A

RESOLUTION

WHEREAS, Town A has limited capability to undertake extensive participation in the preparation of a hazard mitigation plan; and.

WHEREAS, X is able to act on behalf of Town A in the analysis and development of a hazard mitigation plan; and

WHEREAS, X shall prepare a hazard mitigation plan in accordance with 44 FEMA requirements at 44 C.F.R. 201.6; and

WHEREAS, X shall deliver a draft copy of the Plan for public comment as well as the governing body's comment during the planning process and prior to adoption.

NOW THEREFORE, Town Council authorizes X on behalf of Town A to prepare the County ABC Multi-Hazard Mitigation Plan, which shall be reviewed and considered for adoption by Town Council upon completion.

ADOPTED this XX day of December, 20XX at the meeting of the Town Council.

_____
(Mayor)

Tip 12 – Satisfactory participation before appointing Authorized Representative

Appoint the authorized representative at the start of the planning process. Unless the jurisdiction has completed satisfactory participation up to the point of appointing an authorized representative, it will not satisfy the requirements for participation.

Combination Model

Some plans have been prepared with a combination of Direct Representation and Authorized Representation, especially for plans with relatively large numbers of jurisdictions where there is a range of capabilities among the jurisdictions.

For instance, one combination could be the following. Led by a Plan Author, the jurisdictions may, due to large numbers, be divided into several sub-groups, perhaps by geographic proximity or some other common characteristic or interest. Larger jurisdictions may have direct representation on the Planning Team. Each of the sub-groups may authorize a Representative to act on their behalf, similar to the Authorized Representation model described earlier. The sub-group of Authorized Representatives, combined with any direct representatives, then constitutes the Planning Team for development of the plan which is directed, coordinated, or managed by the Plan Author (see Figure 4).

An example of such a situation would be where a county provides the overall leadership and relies upon Councils of Government (COGs) to represent the smaller jurisdictions, and the larger cities have direct representation.

In order to unquestionably meet the participation criteria, each jurisdiction should formally authorize the Plan Author to act on their behalf in the development of the plan.

Any reasonable way to organize the participants will be acceptable if the jurisdiction demonstrates some kind of direct or representative participation. Make sure the plan clearly describes jurisdictional representation or formally authorized representation in the process.

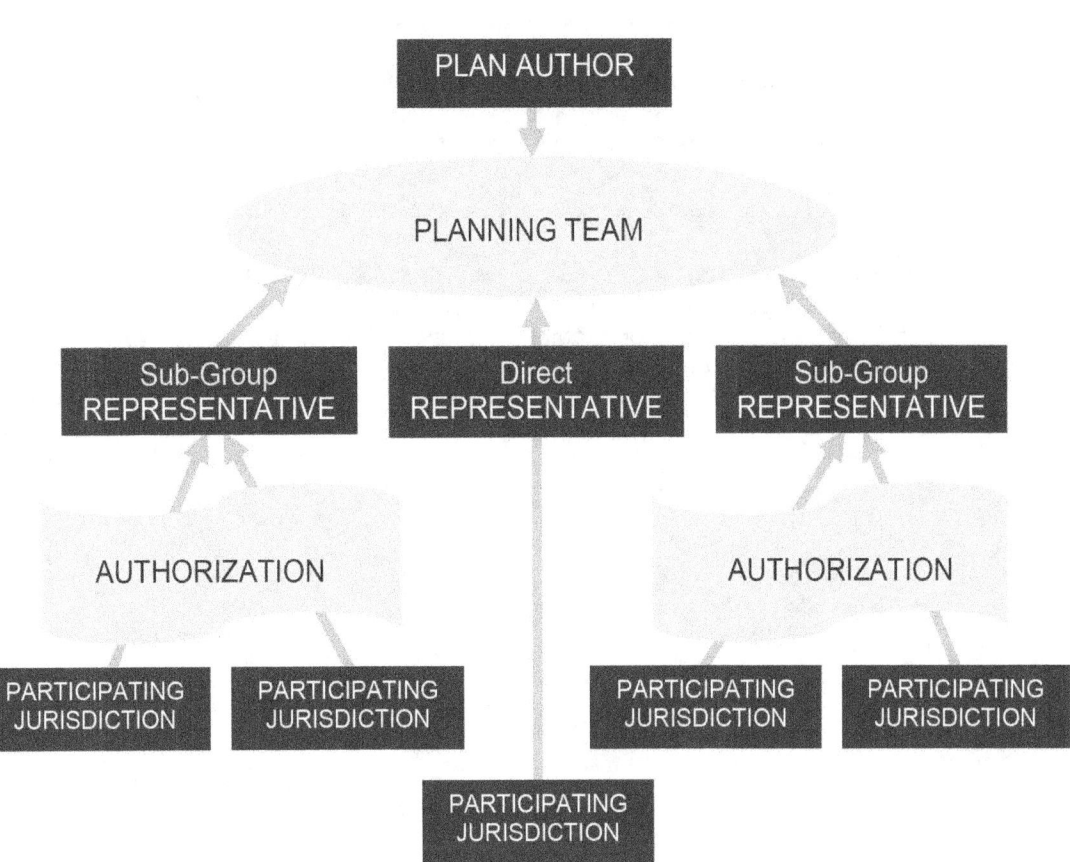

Figure 4. Combination Model

TIP 13 – Define participation

The Plan Author or Planning Team should explicitly define what will constitute satisfactory participation at the start of the process.

In the Authorized Representation model, the measure of satisfactory participation could be that the participating jurisdictions formally authorize the Plan Author to develop the plan.

With direct or indirect representation, satisfactory participation should reflect the amount of interaction deemed appropriate to make the plan reflective of participants' needs and interests. Some measures that could be used include:

- Attendance at a specified number of meetings or work sessions,
- Submission of requested data,
- Response to interviews,
- Review and comment on draft materials,
- Hosting opportunities for public involvement, and

- Linking local Web sites to a plan Web site.

Include in the plan a description of what constitutes satisfactory participation and a record of whether each participant qualified. A simple tool to document this would be a table such as that shown in Exhibit 3.

Establish the measures of satisfactory participation early and stick to them. These measures will allow the plan to stay on schedule if the Planning Team/Plan Author is not waiting for tardy participants.

Remember, this discussion applies to the involvement of each jurisdiction in the planning process. The plan still needs to contain all the required elements of the plan for each jurisdiction (for example, identification of unique hazards, risks, mitigation goals, actions, etc.).

Sample Exhibit 3: Record of Participation

The Planning Team determined that only those jurisdictions that meet all the participation components (listed in Table X) will be considered as a "participating jurisdiction" in this hazard mitigation plan.

Table X. Record of Participation

Nature of Participation	Town A	Town B	Village C
Attended meetings or work sessions (a minimum of 2 meetings will be considered satisfactory).	◼	▨	◼
Submitted inventory and summary of reports and plans relevant to hazard mitigation.	◼	▨	◼
Submitted list of hazards that affect the jurisdiction.	◼	◼	◼
Submitted description of what is at risk (including local critical facilities and infrastructure at risk from which hazards).	◼	◼	◼
Submitted a description or map of local land-use patterns (current and proposed/expected).	◼	◼	◼
Developed goals for the community.	◼	▨	◼
Developed mitigation actions with an analysis/explanation of why those actions were selected.	◼	▨	◼
Prioritized actions emphasizing relative cost-effectiveness.	◼	▨	◼
Completed questionnaires (with implementation strategy).	◼	▨	◼
Reviewed and commented on draft Plan.	◼	◼	◼
Hosted opportunities for public involvement (for example, linking local internet presence to a Plan Web site).	◼	◼	◼

◼ Met

▨ Not met

According to the participation components set by the Planning Team, only Town A and Village C have met the satisfactory participation requirements of this hazard mitigation plan.

TIP 14 – What if some jurisdictions do not qualify for satisfactory participation?

It is possible that some of the participants will not qualify for satisfactory participation, as defined in the plan. To accommodate participants that are non-satisfactory in one or more of the participation components, the jurisdiction may select the most appropriate option from the following suggestions:

- Join the plan during the Plan Maintenance cycle before the next formal Plan Update (for example, the 1-year review). The plan should specify how participation can occur in the Plan Maintenance section. In addition, jurisdictions should consult with their SHMO to determine what steps must be taken to comply with FEMA procedures for adding a jurisdiction to an approved plan.
- Join the plan during the regular plan update cycle (for example, the 5-year update).
- Extract data and material directly from the multi-jurisdictional plan to prepare its own single jurisdiction plan.

Step 4 of the FEMA publication, *Developing the Mitigation Plan: Identifying Mitigation Actions and Implementation Strategies* (FEMA 386-3), explains how to document the planning process.

Documentation of the Planning Process

Plan Review Evaluation Criteria

*Requirement §201.6(b): In order to develop a more comprehensive approach to reducing the effects of natural disasters, the planning process **shall** include:*

(1) An opportunity for the public to comment on the plan during the drafting stage and prior to plan approval;

(2) An opportunity for neighboring jurisdictions, local and regional agencies involved in hazard mitigation activities, and agencies that have the authority to regulate development, as well as businesses, academia and other private and non-profit interests to be involved in the planning process; and,

(3) Review and incorporation, if appropriate, of existing plans, studies, reports, and technical information.

*Requirement §201.6(c)(1): [The plan **shall** document] the planning process used to develop the plan, including how it was prepared, who was involved in the process, and how the public was involved.*

Element	Typical Reviewer's Comments
A. Does the plan provide a narrative description of the process followed to prepare the plan?	**Required:** • Provide a narrative that summarizes the process used to prepare the plan.
B. Does the plan indicate who was involved in the planning process? (For example, who led the development at the staff level and were there any external contributors such as contractors? Who participated on the plan committee, provided information, reviewed drafts, etc.?)	**Required:** • Describe who was involved in the planning process. **Recommended:** • Include in the description the composition of the [committee/Planning Team]) and how each member contributed to the process (i.e., what was his/her role). Describe who led the development of the plan at the staff level, whether there were external contributors (such as a local university or contractor), and what other interested parties were involved.
C. Does the plan indicate how the public was involved? (Was the public provided an opportunity to comment on the plan during the drafting stage and prior to the plan approval?)	**Required:** • Explain how the public was given the opportunity to comment on the plan during the drafting stage and also prior to plan approval.

Element	Typical Reviewer's Comments
D. Was there an opportunity for neighboring jurisdictions, agencies, businesses, academia, nonprofits, and other interested parties to be involved in the planning process?	**Required:** ▪ Discuss how local, State, and Federal agencies, neighboring jurisdictions, local businesses, community leaders, educators, and other relevant private and nonprofit interest groups participated in the plan development.
E. Does the planning process describe the review and incorporation, if appropriate, of existing plans, studies, reports, and technical information?	**Required:** ▪ Describe how existing plans, studies, reports, and technical documents were reviewed and integrated in the planning process.

TIP 15 – Provide opportunity for public comment at least twice in the process

At a minimum there must be an opportunity for the public to comment on the plan during the drafting stage and again prior to plan approval.

It is advisable to make the process as open as possible. To this end, provide public comment opportunities at all meetings of the Planning Team.

TIP 16 – Document data reviewed / incorporated

Include a table in the plan similar to Exhibit 4A to summarize efforts to identify, review, and incorporate existing plans, studies, and other technical documents. While not required, it is advisable to show how each jurisdiction's documents were incorporated.

Use a form similar to Exhibit 4B to summarize this effort by jurisdiction. (This exhibit could be used to meet one of the components required for satisfactory participation.) This table will be useful to identify planning mechanisms appropriate in which to incorporate mitigation actions, programs, or policies that are identified in the plan. This is required later in the crosswalk.

Incorporate data in the Hazard Identification, Hazard Profile, Risk Assessment, Mitigation Actions, or other sections of the plan as applicable to the jurisdiction. To demonstrate incorporation of the material into the plan, insert a notation in the Table, as in Exhibit 4A, indicating where in the plan the information is reflected.

Sample Exhibit 4A: Record of Review
Record of the review and incorporation of existing programs, policies, and technical documents for a single local jurisdiction

(Name of Jurisdiction) ___Town A_____

Existing Program/ Policy/ Technical Documents	Does the jurisdiction have this program/ policy/ technical document? (Yes/No)	Reviewed? (Yes/No)	Method of incorporation into the hazard mitigation plan
Comprehensive Plan	Yes	Yes	Used for assessing development trends and future vulnerabilities
Growth Management Plan	No	No	
Capital Improvement Plan/Program	No	No	
Flood Damage Prevention Ordinance	No	No	
Floodplain Management Plan	Yes	Yes	Incorporated actions
Flood Insurance Studies or Engineering studies for streams	Yes	Yes	Incorporated expected frequency and extent of flooding
Hazard Vulnerability Analysis (by the local Emergency Management Agency)	No	No	
Emergency Management Plan	No	No	
Zoning Ordinance	Yes	Yes	Used for assessing future growth
Building Code	No	No	
Drainage Ordinance	No	No	
Critical Facilities maps	No	No	
Existing Land Use maps	Yes	Yes	Used for assessing vulnerability
Elevation Certificates	No	No	
State Plan	Yes	Yes	Incorporated risk assessment data
HAZUS	Yes	Yes	Used for loss estimation

Prepared by:

Name _____

Title _____

Telephone _____

Sample Exhibit 4B: Record of Review (Summary)
Record of the review of existing programs, policies, and technical documents for all participating jurisdictions

Existing Program/ Policy/ Technical Documents	Town A	Town B	Village C
Comprehensive Plan	NA	0	NA
Growth Management Plan	NA	√	√
Flood Damage Prevention Ordinance	NA	NA	√
Floodplain Management Plan	√	NA	√
Flood Insurance Studies or Engineering studies for streams	0	√	NA
Hazard Vulnerability Analysis (by the local Emergency Management Agency)	NA	0	√
Emergency Management Plan	NA	√	0
Zoning Ordinance	√	0	0
Building Code	NA	√	NA
Drainage Ordinance	NA	NA	√
Critical Facilities maps	NA	√	0
Existing Land Use maps	√	√	√
Elevation Certificates	NA	NA	√
State Plan	√	0	0
HAZUS	√	√	NA

Key:

NA   = the jurisdiction does not have this program/policy/technical document
0   = the jurisdiction has the program/policy/technical document, but did not review/incorporate it into the multi-hazard mitigation plan
√   = the jurisdiction reviewed the program/policy/technical document

Refer to the FEMA publication, *Understanding Your Risks: Identifying Hazards and Estimating Losses* (FEMA 386-2) for guidance in conducting a risk assessment.

Plan Review Evaluation Criteria

Requirement §201.6(c)(2): *The plan shall include a risk assessment that provides the factual basis for activities proposed in the strategy to reduce losses from identified hazards. Local risk assessments must provide sufficient information to enable the jurisdiction to identify and prioritize appropriate mitigation actions to reduce losses from identified hazards.*

Identifying Hazards

Plan Review Evaluation Criteria

Requirement §201.6(c)(2)(i): *[The risk assessment **shall** include a] description of the type ... of all natural hazards that can affect the jurisdiction.*

Element	Typical Reviewer's Comments
A. Does the plan include a description of the types of all natural hazards that affect the jurisdiction? If the hazard identification omits (without explanation) any hazards commonly recognized as threats to the jurisdiction, this part of the plan cannot receive a Satisfactory score.	**Required** • Identify all natural hazards that affect <u>each</u> jurisdiction.

TIP 17 – List all possible hazards

To demonstrate that the planning process included consideration of all potential hazards, include a list of all the hazards identified. Indicate which hazards were deemed to be applicable. Prepare a summary table like that shown in Exhibit 5, showing the universe of hazards considered, including the ones that may not affect specific jurisdictions.

TIP 18 – Consult the State hazard mitigation plan when identifying hazards

Your State hazard mitigation plan lists the hazards that can potentially occur in your planning area. Clearly indicate that you consulted the State hazard mitigation plan in identifying the hazards. For consistency purposes, use the same hazard names as listed in the State hazard mitigation plan.

TIP 19 – Identify and describe the common hazards

Identify which hazards affect all jurisdictions. These may include hazards like hail, lightning, or tornadoes, which normally do not have specific areas of occurrence.

TIP 20 – Identify and describe hazards that vary by jurisdiction

Indicate which geographically specific hazards affect specific jurisdictions. It may be possible that a hazard constitutes a significant risk to some jurisdictions and not others. Summarizing the data in a table (see Exhibit 5 below) can be instrumental in helping each jurisdiction focus on its most important hazards.

TIP 21 – Differentiate between hazards

Avoid combining dissimilar hazards like drought and heat. These hazards may occur at the same time, but they are different in effect and mitigation solutions. Similarly, flooding occurs in a variety of hazard types. Differentiate between storm surge or tidal flooding, riverine flooding, flash flooding, and urban flooding. Each type of flooding has different causes and potentially different mitigation choices.

Differentiate between weather events and the hazards caused by the event. For example, a hurricane causes the specific hazards of high wind, storm surge, and coastal flooding, and each hazard needs to be profiled individually in order to develop appropriate mitigation solutions.

Sample Exhibit 5: Hazard Identification by Jurisdiction

Natural Hazards Considered	Town A	Town B	Village C	Town D
Flash Floods	√	√	√	NA
Landslides	√	√	√	√
Tornadoes	√	√	√	√
Drought	√	√	√	√
Dam failure	NA	√	NA	NA
Extreme heat	√	√	√	√
Wildfire	√	√	√	√

Key

√   = Affects the jurisdiction
NA   = Not a hazard to the jurisdiction

Profiling Hazards

Plan Review Evaluation Criteria

*Requirement §201.6(c)(2)(i): [The risk assessment **shall** include a] description of the ... location and extent of all natural hazards that can affect <u>the jurisdiction</u>. The plan **shall** include information on previous occurrences of hazard events and on the probability of future hazard events.*

Element	Typical Reviewer's Comments
A. Does the risk assessment identify the location (i.e., geographic area affected) of each natural hazard addressed in the plan?	**Required** ▪ For geographically specific hazards, describe the location of the hazard in <u>each</u> jurisdiction. ▪ For hazards that can affect any location in all of the participating jurisdictions, include a statement to that effect.
B. Does the risk assessment identify the extent (i.e., magnitude or severity) of each hazard addressed in the plan?	**Required** ▪ For geographically specific hazards, describe the extent of the hazard <u>by</u> jurisdiction. ▪ For hazards that have uniform extent for all the participating jurisdictions, include a statement to that effect.
C. Does the plan provide information on previous occurrences of each hazard addressed in the plan?	**Required** ▪ Describe previous occurrences <u>by</u> jurisdiction.
D. Does the plan include the probability of future events (i.e., chance of occurrence) for each hazard addressed in the plan?	**Required** ▪ For geographically specific hazards, describe the probability of future events <u>by</u> jurisdiction. ▪ For hazards that have the same probability of future occurrence for all the participating jurisdictions, include a statement to that effect.

TIP 22 – Use maps at appropriate scales

Maps are an excellent way to clearly identify the location of the hazard in each affected jurisdiction. When preparing maps, use a scale that is appropriate to convey the information. Also, when data are available, include on the map land uses, buildings, critical facilities, and other infrastructure located in hazard areas. Some additional tips to keep in mind when preparing maps include:

- Establish mapping standards early in the planning process.
- Use uniform land use designations for all jurisdictions.
- Show jurisdictional boundaries on all maps. Avoid maps that show areas well beyond the geographic extent of the plan.
- Use maps that can be reproduced in black and white without losing legibility.
- Provide a title and legend as appropriate for all maps.

TIP 23 – Address area-wide hazards

For hazards that affect the entire geographical area covered by the plan, include a statement that these hazards affect the entire planning area. Similarly, if the hazard's extent and probability of future occurrence is expected to be the same for all jurisdictions, include a statement to that effect. Be sure this is consistent with other information in the plan. The plan would still need to include the history of each hazard for each jurisdiction.

TIP 24 – Use separate write-ups for each jurisdiction's hazard profiles

Use a separate write-up for each jurisdiction's hazard profiles discussing the location, extent, history, and probability of future occurrences for each geographically specific hazard affecting the jurisdiction.

If the plan lacks data regarding a certain aspect of a geographically specific hazard (location, extent, history, or probability of future occurrences), the plan should mention which jurisdictions lack what kind of data. Those jurisdictions can then formulate actions in the mitigation strategy section to address those data limitations as part of the plan update process.

TIP 25 – Address hazards that can have common solutions for multiple jurisdictions

For hazards that affect multiple jurisdictions (e.g., flooding), a common profile description (in addition to the jurisdiction-specific profiles) is appropriate so that opportunities to develop multi-jurisdictional mitigation solutions become clear.

Assessing Vulnerability: Overview

Plan Review Evaluation Criteria

*Requirement §201.6(c)(2)(ii): [The risk assessment **shall** include a] description of <u>the jurisdiction's</u> vulnerability to the hazards described in paragraph (c)(2)(i) of this section. This description **shall** include an overall summary of each hazard and its impact on the community.*

Element	Typical Reviewer's Comments
A. Does the plan include an overall summary description of the jurisdiction's vulnerability to each hazard?	**Required** ▪ Describe <u>each</u> jurisdiction's vulnerability to each identified hazard. **Recommended** ▪ Provide a matrix with hazards on one axis and jurisdictions on the other axis, and indicate where high, medium, low, and no vulnerability exist.
B. Does the plan address the impact of each hazard on the jurisdiction?	**Required** ▪ For <u>each</u> jurisdiction describe the hazard's impact (for example, type and extent of damage to buildings, infrastructure, critical facilities, and activities, including evacuation and emergency services).

TIP 26 – Summarize overall vulnerability and impact of hazards on each jurisdiction

Have each jurisdiction complete the following steps:
▪ Examine the hazard maps that show their jurisdiction and identify the areas that could be adversely affected by each hazard.
▪ Describe what might happen. Describe the likely result of a hazard occurrence to the jurisdiction. Go on to rank the effects from least to most impact.
See Exhibit 6 for an example.

Sample Exhibit 6: Overall Summary of Vulnerability by Jurisdiction

Natural Hazards Identified	Town A	Town B	Village C	Town D
Flash floods	H	M	L	NA
Landslides	L	H	L	M
Tornadoes	M	M	M	H
Drought	L	L	H	L
Dam failure	NA	H	NA	NA
Extreme heat	M	M	M	M
Wildfire	H	M	M	L

Key
(Definitions below are only an example; jurisdictions may create their own ranking system.)

NA	= Not applicable; not a hazard to the jurisdiction
L	= Low risk; little damage potential (for example, minor damage to less than 5% of the jurisdiction)
M	= Medium risk; moderate damage potential (for example, causing partial damage to 5-10% of the jurisdiction, infrequent occurrence)
H	= High risk; significant risk/major damage potential (for example, destructive, damage to more than 10% of the jurisdiction, regular occurrence)

Assessing Vulnerability: Identifying Structures

Plan Review Evaluation Criteria

Requirement §201.6(c)(2)(ii)(A): *The plan* **should** *describe vulnerability in terms of the types and numbers of existing and future buildings, infrastructure, and critical facilities located in the identified hazard area ... .*

Element	Typical Reviewer's Comments
A. Does the plan describe vulnerability in terms of the types and numbers of existing buildings, infrastructure, and critical facilities located in the identified hazard areas?	*Note: A "Needs Improvement" score on this requirement will not preclude the plan from being approved.* **Recommended** ▪ For all identified hazards, identify the type and number of existing buildings, infrastructure, and critical facilities within each hazard area in <u>each</u> jurisdiction. ▪ Identify the kinds of buildings (for example, residential, commercial, institutional, recreational, industrial, and municipal); infrastructure, (for example, roadways, bridges, utilities, and communications systems); and critical facilities (for example, shelters, hospitals, police, and fire stations) in each jurisdiction.
B. Does the plan describe vulnerability in terms of the types and numbers of future buildings, infrastructure, and critical facilities located in the identified hazard areas?	*Note: A "Needs Improvement" score on this requirement will not preclude the plan from being approved.* **Recommended** ▪ For all identified hazards, identify the type and number of future buildings, infrastructure, and critical facilities within each hazard area for <u>each</u> jurisdiction.

TIP 27 – Differentiate between exposure and vulnerability

Remember that simple exposure to a hazard does not mean a structure is vulnerable. For example, a structure exposed to high winds on the coast may not be damaged by winds if it is built to code to withstand those high winds. Differentiate between those assets that may be damaged from those that are not likely to be adversely affected.

TIP 28 – Estimate future vulnerability

Identify on a map where future development may occur based on local zoning, land use, or comprehensive plans, or simply based on an "educated guess" that extrapolates past development trends. Compare the identified locations to the hazard maps to show where future problems may occur.

Use best judgment to estimate how much development of various land uses and infrastructure would be at risk. For this exercise, project growth for some nominal period (for example, 10 years) to create an estimate of the number of buildings, etc., that could be at future risk.

Assessing Vulnerability: Estimating Potential Losses

Plan Review Evaluation Criteria

*Requirement §201.6(c)(2)(ii)(B): [The plan **should** describe vulnerability in terms of an] estimate of the potential dollar losses to vulnerable structures identified in paragraph (c)(2)(i)(A) of this section and a description of the methodology used to prepare the estimate ... .*

Element	Typical Reviewer's Comments
A. Does the plan estimate potential dollar losses to vulnerable structures?	*Note: A "Needs Improvement" score on this requirement will not preclude the plan from being approved.* **Recommended** ▪ Describe vulnerability in terms of estimated potential dollar losses for each identified hazard for <u>each</u> jurisdiction.
B Does the plan describe the methodology used to prepare the estimate?	*Note: A "Needs Improvement" score on this requirement will not preclude the plan from being approved.* **Recommended** ▪ Describe the methodology used to estimate losses.

TIP 29 – Estimate potential dollar losses

Refer to Step 4 of FEMA's *Understanding Your Risks: Identifying Hazards and Estimating Losses* (FEMA 386-2) and fill out the worksheets from that section for each participating jurisdiction.

Assessing Vulnerability: Analyzing Development Trends

Plan Review Evaluation Criteria

*Requirement §201.6(c)(2)(ii)(C): [The plan **should** describe vulnerability in terms of] providing a general description of land uses and development trends within the community so that mitigation options can be considered in future land use decisions.*

Element	Typical Reviewer's Comments
A. Does the plan describe land uses and development trends?	*Note: A "Needs Improvement" score on this requirement will not preclude the plan from being approved.* **Recommended** ▪ Provide a general overview of land uses (for example, location and kind of use) for each jurisdiction. ▪ Describe development trends occurring within each jurisdiction (for example, describe the types of development occurring, location, density, and growth rate).

TIP 30 – Use maps

Before conducting the vulnerability assessment, prepare maps showing land use, infrastructure, and critical facility data to assist the Planning Team in carrying out this part of the planning process.

TIP 31 – Show development trends

Describe trends in terms of amount of change over time (for example, number of houses/year) and identify where the development is occurring.

Differentiate land uses of similar types that have distinctly different densities (for example, single-family homes, attached housing, and multifamily housing).

Show where the future land uses are likely to occur based on comprehensive plans, zoning, or simply an extension of historic patterns.

Show the expected growth or redevelopment for some reasonable future timeframe (for example, 10 years).

Multi-Jurisdictional Risk Assessment

Plan Review Evaluation Criteria

*Requirement §201.6(c)(2)(iii): For multi-jurisdictional plans, the risk assessment **must** assess <u>each jurisdiction's</u> risks where they vary from the risks facing the entire planning area.*

Element	Typical Reviewer's Comments
A. Does the plan include a risk assessment for each participating jurisdiction as needed to reflect unique or varied risks?	**Required** ▪ For <u>each</u> jurisdiction, identify and assess all risks that are not common to the entire planning area. **Recommended** ▪ Prepare a matrix of the various jurisdictions and the range of hazards to show which risks are common and which are unique.

TIP 32 – Identify unique risks to each jurisdiction

Some risks are common and a range of mitigation actions can be developed for consideration by all jurisdictions. Other risks have geographically specific limits, affecting some jurisdictions more than others. For example, two towns may lie adjacent to each other. One town is older and was a river port, with much development in the floodplain. Its neighbor, more recently developed, has zoned the floodplain for open space. The two towns have a similar hazard (flooding), but very different risks. Provide separate descriptions of the risks for each jurisdiction. Describe the particular areas, populations, and structures that are at risk from each hazard.

The FEMA publication, *Developing the Mitigation Plan: Identifying Mitigation Actions and Implementation Strategies* (FEMA 386-3), discusses in detail how to formulate goals, objectives, and actions, prioritize the actions, and devise an implementation strategy.

Requirement §201.6(c)(3): The plan shall include a mitigation strategy that provides the jurisdiction's blueprint for reducing the potential losses identified in the risk assessment, based on existing authorities, policies, programs and resources, and its ability to expand on and improve these existing tools.

Local Hazard Mitigation Goals

Plan Review Evaluation Criteria

Requirement §201.6(c)(3)(i): [The hazard mitigation strategy shall include a] description of mitigation goals to reduce or avoid long-term vulnerabilities to the identified hazards.

Element	Typical Reviewer's Comments
A Does the plan include a description of mitigation goals to reduce or avoid long-term vulnerabilities to the identified hazards? (Goals are long-term; represent what the community wants to achieve, such as "eliminate flood damage"; and are based on the risk assessment findings.)	**Required** ▪ Describe the hazard reduction goals to reduce or avoid hazard vulnerabilities for each jurisdiction.

TIP 33 – Develop goals that address specific risks

From the jurisdiction's risk assessment and description of past impacts, identify goals for each jurisdiction that address risks applicable to each hazard.

Avoid overly general goals or goals that are common to all hazards. Well-defined goals will lead to effective actions.

Identification and Analysis of Mitigation Actions

Plan Review Evaluation Criteria

*Requirement §201.6(c)(3)(ii): [The mitigation strategy **shall** include a] section that identifies and analyzes a comprehensive range of specific mitigation actions and projects being considered to reduce the effects of each hazard, with particular emphasis on new and existing buildings and infrastructure.*

Element	Typical Reviewer's Comments
A. Does the plan identify and analyze a comprehensive range of specific mitigation actions and projects for each hazard?	**Required** ▪ Identify and analyze a comprehensive range of specific mitigation actions for each hazard for each jurisdiction.
B Do the identified actions and projects address reducing the effects of hazards on new buildings and infrastructure?	**Required** ▪ Develop actions that address the effects of hazards on new buildings and infrastructure in each jurisdiction. **Recommended** ▪ Develop a matrix to show what actions address specific hazards and new buildings and infrastructure. The matrix should also address which communities are covered by the actions.
C. Do the identified actions and projects address reducing the effects of hazards on existing buildings and infrastructure?	**Required** ▪ Develop actions that address the effects of hazards on existing buildings and infrastructure in each jurisdiction. **Recommended** ▪ Develop a matrix to show what actions address specific hazards and existing buildings and infrastructure. The matrix should also show which communities are covered by the actions.

TIP 34 – Select appropriate actions for each jurisdiction

Describing a comprehensive range of actions is best done as part of the hazard profile section. The description could consist of a list of possible mitigation responses to a particular hazard. Then, select from those actions the ones that best address each jurisdiction's vulnerability, capabilities, and interests.

Document the "evaluation" of the range of actions using Worksheet 4 of *Developing the Mitigation Plan: Identifying Mitigation Actions and Implementation Strategies* (FEMA 386-3).

TIP 35 – Address new and existing buildings and infrastructure

Make sure that the action or actions address <u>both</u> new and existing buildings and infrastructure (see Exhibit 7).

Implementation of Mitigation Actions (Multi-Jurisdictional Mitigation Actions)

Plan Review Evaluation Criteria

*Requirement §201.6(c)(3)(iv): For multi-jurisdictional plans, there **must** be identifiable action items specific to the jurisdiction requesting FEMA approval or credit of the plan.*

Element	Typical Reviewer's Comments
A Does the plan include at least one identifiable action item for each jurisdiction requesting FEMA approval of the plan?	**Required** • Identify at least one mitigation action per jurisdiction (see Exhibit 7).

Sample Exhibit 7: Actions by Jurisdiction

Mitigation Actions	Applicable to New / Existing Buildings and Infrastructure	Town A	Town B	Village C	Town D
Bridge Replacement (elevate above BFE)	Existing	√			
Repetitive Loss Property Acquisition	Existing	√		√	√
Elevate critical facility above BFE	Existing	√			√
Public awareness program on local TV channel for tornado safety	New and existing	√	√		√
Code Update	New	√	√	√	√
Construct safe rooms in ABC neighborhood	Existing		√		

Key
√   = The jurisdiction will implement this action

*Requirement: §201.6(c)(3)(iii): [The mitigation strategy section **shall** include] an action plan describing how the actions identified in section (c)(3)(ii) will be prioritized, implemented, and administered by the local jurisdiction. Prioritization **shall** include a special emphasis on the extent to which benefits are maximized according to a cost benefit review of the proposed projects and their associated costs.*

Element	Typical Reviewer's Comments
A. Does the mitigation strategy include how the actions are prioritized? (For example, is there a discussion of the process and criteria used?)	**Required** ▪ Describe <u>each</u> jurisdiction's method for prioritizing actions. (In addition to cost benefit review, considerations may include social impact, technical feasibility, administrative capabilities, and political and legal effects, as well as environmental issues.)
B. Does the mitigation strategy address how the actions will be implemented and administered? (For example, does it identify the responsible department, existing and potential resources, and timeframe?)	**Required** ▪ Describe how the actions will be implemented and administered by <u>each</u> jurisdiction. Include in the description the responsible party(ies)/agency(ies), the funding source(s), and the target completion dates for each action.
C. Does the prioritization process include an emphasis on the use of a cost-benefit review (see page 3-36 of Multi-Hazard Mitigation Planning Guidance) to maximize benefits?	**Required** ▪ Describe the cost benefit review performed during the prioritization process to identify actions/projects with the greatest benefits. (If cost and benefit data are missing, a qualitative assessment of the comparative benefits will suffice.)

TIP 36 – Include at-least one action and implementation strategy for each jurisdiction

Use Exhibit 8, one for each jurisdiction, to provide a summary of all needed information.

TIP 37 – Identify collaborative actions

Actions by individual jurisdictions may be part of or contribute to an area-wide mitigation action. The scope of such an action may be entirely within the jurisdiction or may be part of a larger action involving some or all of the other jurisdictions covered in the plan.

Sample Exhibit 8: Implementation Strategy

(Name of Jurisdiction)   Town A

Priority*	Mitigation Action/ Program/ Project	Hazard Addressed	Applies to Community Assets (Existing/ New)	Existing Local Planning Mechanism through which the action will be implemented	Primary Agency Responsible for Implementation / for Administration	Date for Completion	Estimated Cost ($)	Funding Source
1.	Bridge Replacement (elevate above BFE)	Flood	Existing	Capital Improvement Plan	Dept of Public Works / DPW Director	2 years from when funds are made available	$90,000	FEMA Public Assistance 406 Mitigation Funds
2.	Repetitive Loss Property Acquisition	Flood	Existing	Floodplain Management Plan	Dept of Public Works / Village Administrator	1 year from when funds are made available	$80,000	Pre-Disaster Mitigation Program (75%) and local match (25%)
3.	Elevate critical facility (hospital) above BFE	Flood	Existing	NFIP participation	NFIP coordinator / Village Administrator	2 years from when funds are made available	$50,000	Flood Mitigation Assistance Program grant
4.	Public awareness program on local TV channel	All	New and existing	NA	Public Outreach Coordinator / County Emergency Management Agency	6 months	$5,000	Private Channel I
5.	Code update	Seismic and wind	New	Building Code Ordinance	Building Department / Planning Director	3 years	Staff time	Department budget

* Priority assigned using a method that emphasized benefit-cost review (see plan text for description).

Prepared by:
Name _____
Title _____
Telephone _____

For plan maintenance, refer to two FEMA publications – *Developing the Mitigation Plan: Identifying Mitigation Actions and Implementation Strategies* (FEMA 386-3) and *Bringing the Plan to Life: Implementing the Hazard Mitigation Plan* (FEMA 386-4). Plan maintenance is not explicitly defined for multi-jurisdictional plans; however, participating communities in the multi-jurisdictional planning process should not rely solely on the lead agency to keep the plan alive. Each participating jurisdiction should have a defined role in maintaining the plan; see the following discussion.

Monitoring, Evaluating, and Updating the Plan

Plan Review Evaluation Criteria

*Requirement §201.6(c)(4)(i): [The plan maintenance process **shall** include a] section describing the method and schedule of monitoring, evaluating, and updating the mitigation plan within a five-year cycle.*

Element	Typical Reviewer's Comments
A. Does the plan describe the method and schedule for monitoring the plan? (For example, does it identify the party responsible for monitoring and include a schedule for reports, site visits, phone calls, and meetings?)	**Required** • Include a description of the method and schedule to monitor the plan. Include in the description the party(s)/agency(s) responsible for ensuring that the monitoring process is accomplished, and how and when the plan will be monitored. **Recommended** • Describe how <u>each</u> jurisdiction will participate in monitoring the plan.
B. Does the plan describe the method and schedule for evaluating the plan? (For example, does it identify the party responsible for evaluating the plan and include the criteria used to evaluate the plan?)	**Required** • Describe the method and schedule to evaluate the plan. Include in the description the party(s)/agency(s) responsible for evaluating the plan, and how and when the plan will be evaluated. **Recommended** • Describe how <u>each</u> jurisdiction will participate in evaluating the plan.
C. Does the plan describe the method and schedule for updating the plan within the five-year cycle?	**Required** • Describe the method and schedule for the plan update. Include in the description the party(s)/agency(s) responsible for updating the plan, and how and when the plan will be updated. **Recommended** • Describe how <u>each</u> jurisdiction will participate in updating the plan.

TIP 38 – Plan to maintain the plan

- If there was a Planning Team, retain it as an ongoing organization to maintain the plan. Replace vacancies at least annually.

- If there was no Planning Team, assign responsibility for coordinating maintenance to the most capable municipal department among the participating jurisdictions. Require that department to acknowledge its role, identifying the individual who will be assigned to oversee the maintenance of the plan. Involve that individual in developing the maintenance strategy for the plan.

- Set a clear schedule (for example, meet annually). Show what needs to be done, when to start, when to meet, who will participate and how, when and how to involve the public, and what conditions require special review/updates.

- As a condition of continuing participation, require each jurisdiction to report on its actions, goals, and changes that may affect the content of the plan.

TIP 39 – Update every 5 years

For multi-jurisdictional plans, the schedule should include a start date early enough to provide each participating jurisdiction adequate time for review, concurrence, adoption, and FEMA approval within the time limit in order to remain eligible for project grant funding.

Incorporation into Existing Planning Mechanisms

Plan Review Evaluation Criteria
*Requirement §201.6(c)(4)(ii): [The plan **shall** include a] process by which <u>local governments</u> incorporate the requirements of the mitigation plan into other planning mechanisms such as comprehensive or capital improvement plans, when appropriate.*

Element	Typical Reviewer's Comments
A. Does the plan identify other local planning mechanisms available for incorporating the requirements of the mitigation plan?	**Required** - Describe applicable local planning mechanisms for each jurisdiction (local planning mechanisms may include comprehensive plans, capital improvement plans, zoning, building codes, site development regulations, permits, and job descriptions).
B. Does the plan include a process by which the local government will incorporate the requirements in other plans, when appropriate?	**Required** - Describe the process to incorporate the mitigation plan requirements into local planning mechanisms for each jurisdiction.

TIP 40 – Identify local planning mechanisms

Local jurisdictions often have varying capabilities and planning mechanisms. Planning mechanisms may include plans, codes, ordinances, regulations, guidelines, and programs. Following are some examples for each of these categories:

Plans
- Comprehensive plans,
- Capital improvement plans,
- Redevelopment plans,
- Area plans,
- Watershed management plans,
- Post-disaster recovery plans,
- Comprehensive emergency management plans,
- Regional development plans, and
- Special functional plans such as:
  - Downtown redevelopment,
  - Airport,
  - Land buyout program,
  - Long-range recreation facilities plan,
  - School siting plan,
  - Open space plan,
  - Transportation improvement/retrofit programs, and
  - Water and sewer construction/retrofit programs.

Codes, Ordinances, Regulations, and Guidelines
- Building codes,
- Land development codes,
- Zoning ordinance,
- Historic preservation ordinance,
- Floodplain ordinance,
- Tree protection ordinance,
- Landscape ordinance,
- Subdivision regulations, and
- Development guidelines.

Programs
- Beach conservation and restoration program,
- Local and/or regional emergency evacuation program, and
- Historic preservation district program.

Using Exhibits 4A and 4B which list some of the more common mechanisms, and the above list, identify in each jurisdiction those planning mechanisms that may be appropriate to use. Develop a matrix of the local planning mechanisms available and indicate how each action could be implemented through them. See Exhibit 8 for a sample format to document this process for each jurisdiction.

TIP 41 – Describe the process for incorporation of plan requirements into other planning or community decision-making processes

For each mechanism, describe how the Hazard Mitigation Plan actions, programs, or policies will be incorporated. For some mechanisms, it may be relatively simple with staff revising the document; for others there may be legislative or executive action required. Briefly describe the process, responsible party, and estimated time to execute the incorporation.

Provide a separate description for each jurisdiction.

Continued Public Involvement

Plan Review Evaluation Criteria

*Requirement §201.6(c)(4)(iii): [The plan maintenance process **shall** include a] discussion on how the community will continue public participation in the plan maintenance process.*

Element	Typical Reviewer's Comments
A. Does the plan explain how continued public participation will be obtained? (For example, will there be public notices, an on-going mitigation plan committee, or annual review meetings with stakeholders?)	**Required** • Describe public participation opportunities that each jurisdiction will have during the plan's monitoring, evaluation, and updates (for example, soliciting input, holding meetings, posting the proposed changes to the plan on the Web, etc.).

TIP 42 – Schedule public involvement

Schedule regular public involvement in the plan maintenance process. Incorporate public involvement into the schedule for the plan maintenance as noted above.

Exhibit 1: Adoption Resolution

(Name of Jurisdiction) _____

(Governing Body) _____

(Address) _____

RESOLUTION

WHEREAS, *(Insert name of Jurisdiction)*, with the assistance from *(Insert name of Plan Author)*, has gathered information and prepared the *(Insert name of the Multi-Jurisdictional Plan)*; and,

WHEREAS, the *(Insert name of the Multi-Jurisdictional Plan)* has been prepared in accordance with FEMA requirements at 44 C.F.R. 201.6; and,

WHEREAS, *(Insert name of Jurisdiction)* is a local unit of government that has afforded the citizens an opportunity to comment and provide input in the Plan and the actions in the Plan; and

WHEREAS, *(Insert the name of the governing body)* has reviewed the Plan and affirms that the Plan will be updated no less than every five years;

NOW THEREFORE, BE IT RESOLVED by *(Insert the name of the governing body)* that *(Insert name of Jurisdiction)* adopts the *(Insert name of the Multi-Jurisdictional Plan)* as this jurisdiction's Multi-Hazard Mitigation Plan, and resolves to execute the actions in the Plan.

ADOPTED this _____ day of _____, 200__ at the meeting of the *(Insert the name of the governing body)*.

Insert appropriate signature lines and dates

_____
(Mayor, Village Clerk, County Board Chair, etc.)

Exhibit 2: Resolution for Authorized Representation

Sample resolution for authorizing the Plan Author to act on behalf of Local Jurisdiction

(Name of Jurisdiction) _____

(Governing Body) _____

(Address) _____

RESOLUTION

WHEREAS, *(Insert name of Jurisdiction)* has limited capability to undertake extensive participation in the preparation of a hazard mitigation plan; and

WHEREAS, *(Insert name of Representative)* is able to act on behalf of *(Insert name of Jurisdiction)* in the analysis and development of a hazard mitigation plan; and

WHEREAS, the *(Insert name of Representative)* shall prepare a hazard mitigation plan in accordance with FEMA requirements at 44 C.F.R. 201.6; and

WHEREAS, *(Insert name of Representative)* shall deliver a draft copy of the Plan for public comment as well as the governing body's comment during the planning process and prior to adoption.

NOW THEREFORE, *(Insert name of the governing body)*, authorizes *(Insert name of Representative)* to (*participate in the preparation* or *prepare*) the *(Insert name of the Multi-Jurisdictional Plan)* on behalf of *(Insert name of Jurisdiction)* which shall be reviewed and considered for adoption by *(Insert name of the governing body)* upon completion.

ADOPTED this _____ day of _____, 200__ at the meeting of the *(Insert the name of the governing body)*.

Insert appropriate signature lines and dates

_____
(Mayor, Village Clerk, County Board Chair, etc.)

Exhibit 3: Record of Participation

Nature and required level of Participation	Insert name of Participating Jurisdiction	Insert name of Participating Jurisdiction	Insert name of Participating Jurisdiction

☐ Met

☐ Not met

Exhibit 4A: Record of Review

Record of the review and incorporation of existing programs, policies, and technical documents for a single local jurisdiction

(Name of Jurisdiction) _____

Existing Program/ Policy/ Technical Documents	Does the jurisdiction have this program/ policy/ technical document? (Yes/No)	Reviewed by Plan Authors? (Yes/No)	Method of incorporation into the hazard mitigation plan

Prepared by:

Name _____

Title _____

Telephone _____

Exhibit 4B: Record of Review (Summary)

Record of the review of existing programs, policies, and technical documents for all participating jurisdictions

Existing Program/ Policy/ Technical Documents	Insert name of Participating Jurisdiction	Insert name of Participating Jurisdiction	Insert name of Participating Jurisdiction

Key

NA = the jurisdiction does not have this program/policy/technical document
0   = the jurisdiction has the program/policy/technical document, but did not review/incorporate it into the multi-hazard mitigation plan
√   = the jurisdiction reviewed the program/policy/technical document

Exhibit 5: Hazard Identification by Jurisdiction

Natural Hazards Considered	Insert name of Participating Jurisdiction	Insert name of Participating Jurisdiction	Insert name of Participating Jurisdiction	Insert name of Participating Jurisdiction
Avalanche *				
Coastal erosion *				
Dam failure *				
Drought				
Earthquake				
Expansive soils *				
Extreme cold				
Extreme heat				
Flash flood *				
Hail				
Ice				
Landslide *				
Levee failure*				
Lightning				
Riverine flooding *				
Snow				
Subsidence *				
Tidal surge *				
Tornado				
Tsunami				
Urban flood *				
Volcano *				
Wildfire *				
Wind (straight line)				
Other				

* These are likely to be geographically specific hazards

Only natural hazards must be considered per the Rule; however, other significant hazards that are manmade should be included as well. See *Integrating Manmade Hazards Into Mitigation Planning* (FEMA 386-7). Additional hazards may include civil unrest, nuclear power plant accidents, non-nuclear power plant accidents, transportation disruptions (port, rail, airport, highways, rivers), use of weapons of mass destruction (nuclear, chemical, biological), and hazardous materials leaks or accidents, etc.

Key

√   = Affects the jurisdiction
NA   = Not a hazard to the jurisdiction

Exhibit 6: Overall Summary of Vulnerability by Jurisdiction

Natural Hazards Identified	Insert name of Participating Jurisdiction	Insert name of Participating Jurisdiction	Insert name of Participating Jurisdiction	Insert name of Participating Jurisdiction

Key
(Define each risk ranking term.)

High =

Medium =

Low =

Exhibit 7: Actions by Jurisdiction

Mitigation Actions	Applicable to New / Existing Buildings and Infrastructure	Insert name of Participating Jurisdiction	Insert name of Participating Jurisdiction	Insert name of Participating Jurisdiction	Insert name of Participating Jurisdiction

Key

√   = The jurisdiction will implement this action

Exhibit 8: Implementation Strategy

(Name of Jurisdiction) _____

Priority	Mitigation Action/ Program/ Project	Hazard Addressed	Applies to Community Assets (Existing/ New)	Existing Local Planning Mechanism through which the action will be implemented	Primary Agency Responsible for Implementation / for Administration	Date for Completion	Estimated Cost ($)	Funding Source

Prepared by:
Name _____
Title _____
Telephone _____